Self Transcending

Noela Paraschiv

Darlos, 2020

Copyright © 2020 by Noela Paraschiv

All rights reserved. No part of this publication may be reproduced, stored, or transmitted in any form or by any means, electronic, mechanical, photocopying, recording, scanning, or otherwise without permission. It is illegal to copy this book, post it to a website, or distribute it by any other means without permission.

ISBN: 978-973-0-33173-8

Illustrations by Teodora Surdu

Self Transcending

to those who know pain,

therefore, to everybody

"The path to paradise begins in hell."

— Dante Alighieri

contents

Hell... **9**

Purgatory **63**

Paradise **125**

Hell

In the darkest of times, <u>Hell</u> rose around her.
She had no chains, yet something bound her to that place...

But somewhere down the line, she'll find the grace to move forward;
she'll leave behind a trace with sadness and sorrow,
despair and deceit, uncertainty and misery
in the journey that would be revelatory...

But until that point, her trajectory
seemed like a walk into the underworld -
hand in hand with the devil himself.

A modern version of Hades and Persephone,
he has seen some of the rougher storms of her life,

                but he created half of them.

Self Transcending

If only I could hear the whispers of my own heart...

Maybe I trained her to keep her mouth shut,
or I've been deaf all along,
one or the other.

But don't get me wrong,
when they told me to follow my heart,

>I actually tried,

>I chased it down the street and further.

Too late I realized that it was yours, not mine.
And it led me to the darkest of places,
but that was just one of the bad phases of my life,

there had been more.

- the art of overthinking -

I'm in a battle with my own mind
daily,
but the saddest thing of all
is that I lose either way.

Negotiating a treaty with the universe,
praying still,
maybe it will stop mocking me,
    making me fight
        against my will.

Quiet sorrow,
always making me quite apathetic.
Do you need a life to borrow?
Cause mine doesn't have an owner
worthy of its custody.

I can offer such a bargain,
an exchange, if you may.
Never felt it was more than *nothing*
        and that's exactly what you'll pay.

Trying to push my limits farther every day,
I always gave my best
in every domain that there is,
but I'm tired of trying to impress
everybody
         but me.

I'm the one who collects
dissatisfaction from all of them, it's tough.
I'm the one who regrets
that my best
         wasn't enough.

"Go out and remove those negative thoughts from your head."

But they could never understand that it takes strength that I don't possess;

I'm lying under a meteor unable to move
cause it dug out my grave.
I'm a mess; my mental state could not improve;
I'm a slave to my depression,
and I haven't got a clue how to save myself.

"Be brave and fight your demons," people say.
But they're locked up in my head,
urging me to choose the easy way out.

So, I need help,
       but there is none in sight.

I just want to live a life without the numbness,
I just want to be set free,
I want less,
cause it's all too much for me.

- memoir of my childhood depression -

I'm not the kind of person that is missed.
I belong in the background of people's lives,
I fit perfectly in the space between the cracks
of an empty haunted house.

No one tries
        to look at me,
        even for a minute,
and I don't condemn them,
        they have their limits
        of tolerance.

I'm unbearable, not worth your energy,
so just leave,
don't waste your time with me.

This scavenger heart of mine
is going to be the death of me.

She welcomes back into our life
each individual who tore it to pieces,
mistakes toxicity for empathy and forgiveness...

How foolish can she be?

*How can it provide a home for trash,
like I'm some kind of garbage bin?*

Drowning my sorrow in tequila glasses
till I can't control my body,
I'm at a party I don't wanna be at.

He pulls me into the boys bathroom,
covering me with kisses,
brutally.

This is not a love story; I'll tell you that.
        This is the story of when I lost my faith in love.

Shoving his hands under my dress,
I don't want this.
I can't stress it enough,

but that's what girls get when caught
        by someone who doesn't perceive
        that *No* is *No*,
and, at that moment,
we just pray that he will leave.

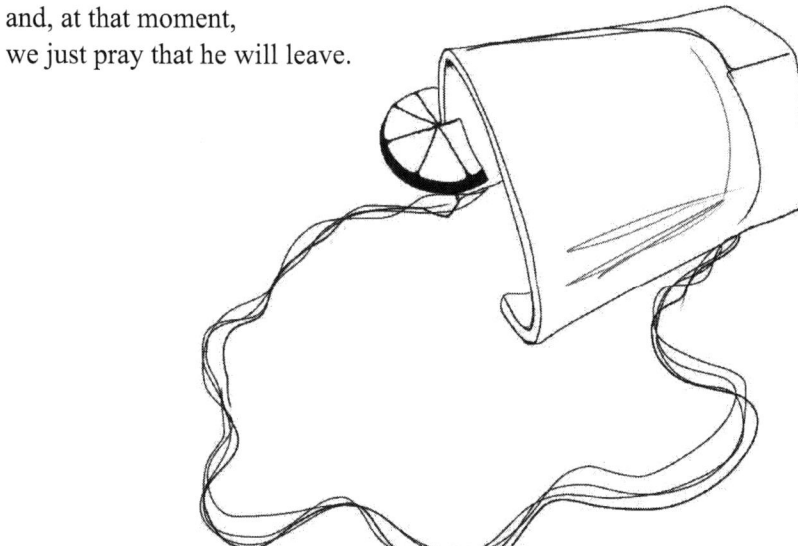

- the tale of failing -

Everything I once knew has vanished into thin air,
but it was never mine to begin with,
I could only hope.

The plot continues with me sobbing for my expectations,
holding onto the hollow of my unfulfilled dreams
with my bare hands,

trying to release it.

But my self-judgment keeps shoving it in my face,
so I can continue to see
everything I was not able to accomplish.

Former friend,

find us standing on a building,
when fear wasn't in our dictionary,

nor was hurting,
                nor was crying,
                              we were revolutionary.

We walked among sick-minded people
and have never caught a cold
cause we were bold enough to stray away from the norm.
It felt like we were born to connect and befriend.

But you left and, eventually, conformed,
so now I am hanging out with mold.

Self Transcending

Memories are coming through,
        but you're not coming back,

so I try to imagine a world without your presence,
I try to fool myself into not remembering.

What a theatrical effort!

Like I don't have an idea what it is that I lack,
like I don't have to suppress your memory
each
      second
            of
                the
                    day,

like it doesn't hurt me anymore.

Midnight thoughts.

My mind wanders miles away nightly

*-never the same direction,
never the same destination-*

but one thing is *constant*:
        always seems to bring you in the picture.

My mind can't forget you're that important,
although I'm still hurt that you picked her.

The feeling never faded out of my body,
but I'm done lying to myself...

I have to accept that it never entered yours.

And, perhaps, it never will,
as much as I'm trying.

Fate prescribed to me a double dosage of love,
        of course it didn't have any left to give to you...

- one-sided love -

I put you on a pedestal without supporting evidence,

but still,
it was a surprise that my expectations hadn't been met.

I could have bet
that you'd be a protagonist in my script.

Turns out you were just another extra...

- the repeated cycle of infatuation -

I keep going back to my old habits...

Although I am trying not to,
I still care about people that forgot about my existence.

Reminiscing,
       but struggling to remember that I count too.

Only some of my memories have persistence,
just happens that the ones involving my worth

                                            are missing.

Often, I speak without making noise...

That must be it
cause I can't spur any reactions
from people around me.

And then, I bump into things,
but it doesn't hurt me
cause I'm without any form of substance.

I travel the land,
don't need no compass.
Where will I land?
No one will know this.

I take directions through divination,
so I have no worries, no woe,
but this is a premiere,
just realized,
I have no feelings at all.

- ghost -

Looking at this body from a distance,
    I used to think it belonged to me.

Misfit.

This isn't my place,
    nor is it my temporary home.

How could it be,
    when I feel alienated from every bone?

Searching for something to hold
cause my spirit is leaving
in an episode of astral projection.

I feel like my life has been sold,

I don't recognize this place,

                this body even.

I'm trapped outside, disconnected,

trying so hard to barge in,
but the steel walls won't let me infiltrate it.

We were as close to love as we'll ever get.

We were puppets,
ruled by our fate,
so we had no say in this…

we fell in love without intentions,
we played along till the play was over,
we had our illusions and expectations painted out,
but then,
        as unexpectedly as they appeared,

we had to let them fade out,
whenever the master puppeteer decided to.

You say, *"let's go back to the 1900s,"*
but then feminism wasn't a thing...

You forgot that my kind barely survived that time?
Don't you remember women were your slaves,
prostitutes, and pets?

A beating replaced the flowers,
they just had to endure it for hours.

Wake up the next morning,
warning:
        you cannot cross their word.
I've heard
        this so many times.
That's what wives
        have to go through...

Let's talk about the Middle East,
where our past is their present,
quite often, there is a feast:
choose a woman, pick a wife,
just take more if you please.

Age doesn't matter,
an entire gender
has to go through slaughter.

Self Transcending

Those canine looking figures
have sharp fangs ready to bite,
one could say, *'they're armed to their teeth'*.
But I'm not intrigued to fight,
       so they should tame their ego.

I am nothing but a stray dog,
       not the competitor type,
       not eager to play that game,
I only strive to stay alive,
       that's my main personal aim.

"Why you never talk about yourself?",
he wondered, in an attempt to gather information.

He was the type that you can trust,
so take the opportunity
                                or suffer eternal damnation.

"*Just open up,*" I encouraged myself,
but words got tangled, and so I couldn't tell...

"It's past my curfew,
I'll stay inside and lock the doors,
don't try and continue,
cause I'll never come outside, and I have no remorse."

                                      - closed off -

Self Transcending

I've squeezed my flesh and bones in every crack
that I could find along the way.

But I never stay.

                                      I always feel wrong.

My curse - endlessly wondering, *"where do I belong?"*

The feeling of not keeping up
keeps my body occupied.

A tenant that doesn't want to leave,
        this thought overstayed way too much.

When the lease runs out,
        it extends its stay.

"I must do more. I must be more."

Will this be permanent?

It may.

Self Transcending

Even with the purest intentions,
I couldn't be any further from my goals...

I am left with no direction
every
single
time
cause I keep losing it all, a repetitive cycle.

I'm stuck in this poorly made recital,
mispronouncing every line...

I am holding constant tryouts - *substitutes* -
in a struggle to feel fine.

Your compassion is appetizing,
and there's plenty of starving creatures downstairs,
ready to stick their fangs onto your flesh
and drain your energy.

No soul cares.

        This is hunger.

                And you're prey.

They won't hesitate to make you suffer,
so take cover if you wanna see another day.

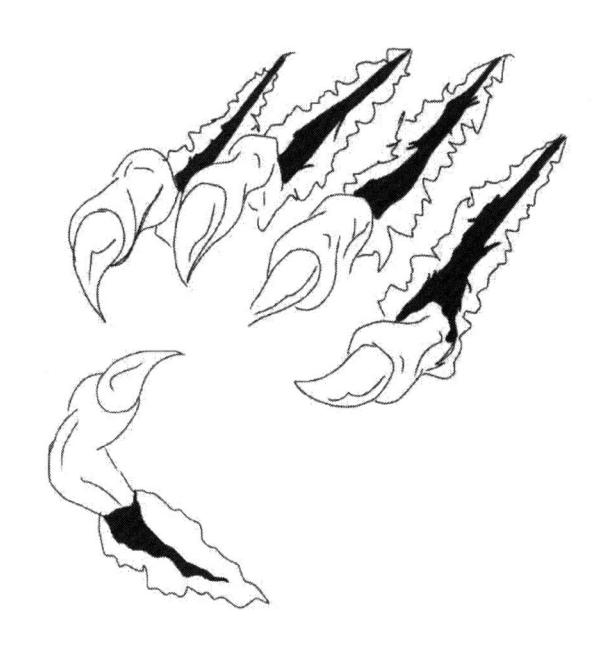

Self Transcending

I can't find my way back home anymore.

He changed locations,
        preferred another's company,
not a pleasant situation,
        though we weren't meant to be.

Certain things didn't align,
lots of miscommunication,
yet he always said, *"I'm fine"*...

It all happened in a second.

Now, I learned my lesson -
never make a home out of a person.

Bloody footprints left behind me,
evidence
for the murder of my soul.

There was no battle to see,
       a premeditated crime,
              and only one suspect: *me.*

- an insight into society's point of view -

You can hold on to your opinion,
                you're way too talkative.
Sometimes it's cute, but now you're acting like a brat.

And stop overreacting!
Your outfit was provocative,
                you were asking for attention.

Know your place: you're *our* possession.
In fact, I'd like you to be more natural.

Oh... but not like that!
You better lose that belly fat,
your body is disgusting...

You say you feel misunderstood:

                              welcome to womanhood.

From a tender age,
I tried to avoid
the very thing that was closest to me,

I learned that I could use objection.

Trying to escape that cage became my obsession,
I wanted to break free
       so much that I've gone insane.

So how come we and our monsters
become one and the same?

Self Transcending

Continuously trying to belong somewhere.

I made peace with the truth:
this is not my place,
even though, pretending,
I put on a mask, not thin.

So I'm trying to recover my colors
because I made the mistake
of hiding my own self behind the borders,

                              in order to fit in.

Burning lives and screaming cries,

picture of the inferno.

It's long-overdue to realize the danger
cause, once upon a time, we had a home,
but we lost a bet with Mother Nature,
          now everything is gone.

There's collective suffering between us,
but it's way too late for prayers,
similar to what you did -
          no one sees, no one knows, no one cares.

This city makes me feel so small.

And these narrow-minded citizens
   are obstructing my pathway out of here.

I often fight with the shackles they placed on my thinking,
but it's quite hard to do that when you grew up in a place where dreams are meant for sleeping.

Their discouragement and laughter is weighing me down,
   and *I just want to get out of this town,*
    and see the possibilities of becoming somebody
      someplace else.

- born in the wrong place -

Twisted words implemented in my mind,
how foolish I was.

You were anything but kind to me,
and I was easily manipulated.
Like candy in your mouth,
your lies, I took them all for granted
cause you sold them in a sweet package,
and now I'm sobbing on the bathroom floor,
a wreckage.

'I'm empty,I lost a big part from within,'
       that's what I thought for months,

but in reality,
       common sense is what I lack.

I know I shouldn't,
       but I still want you to come back.

People don't love with the same intensity,
I've learned this the hard way.

I was just a liability
to them.

For me, *they were reasons to pray.*

Wish I could stop the autopilot that governs my life
and jump out of the viewer's place right into the match
cause I know I'll regret it if I let it pass me by,
and there are infinite things I'd like to do before I die.

But living is a stranger to me,
       wish someone could introduce us
cause I don't have the energy to be excited or content,
and it's not that fun in the end
to be able to detach from every person, every friend,
at any given minute in time.

I know I should care more,
and it works in theory,
but practically, everything I experience is a real bore.
I keep doing things, but I'm not present...

Can't stop feeling like a little peasant,
       property of the universe itself.

- existing -

Our love was doomed to end.
We couldn't have foreseen it, but now, we can't pretend...

From what we had, we only saw bright parts,
our sight was blurry from the heat made by our hearts,
and since we're forced now to part ways,
I just hope we'll reconnect, maybe in another space
or another place in time.

But let's not make presumptions
on something so uncertain,
I don't have expectations
for a common destination in the end
cause incurable optimism has led us to the edge.

But, still, I'll keep you in my heart. *I pledge.*

I couldn't wake you up.

How could I?
You're in a trance of nihilism and nothingness.

How could I light up your whole world
with nothing but a flare,
with you still choosing to look at the blackness,
with you not cooperating but opposing all my views?

How could I teach you to fly
with you cutting down my wings?

How could you say you love me
when there's nothing that you love about life,
when you're sucking the life out of me?

And how could I let you sit in your pile of pessimism
without trying to help,

without getting myself in there as well?

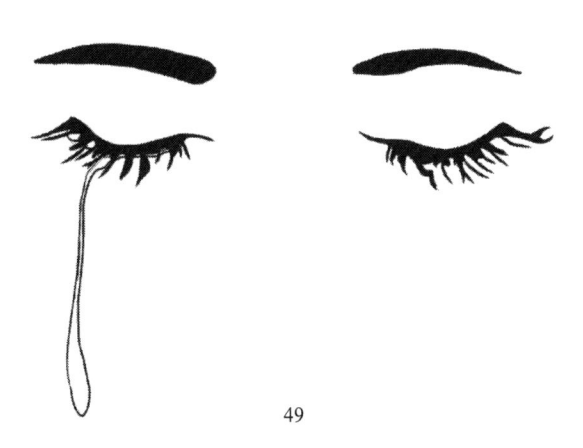

Experts say it takes 18 to 254 days to break a habit,
it's just plain science.

But it's been 3 years now,
and my heart still aches for your presence.

Tell them to revise it, *they are wrong.*

My life has been on hold since I was born;
still waiting, maybe it will begin soon...
I never felt a thing, except alone,
so I'm still wondering, how does living feel?

Well, maybe I have high expectations
that simply cannot be met
or maybe, I'm just waiting for directions,
something that I will never get.

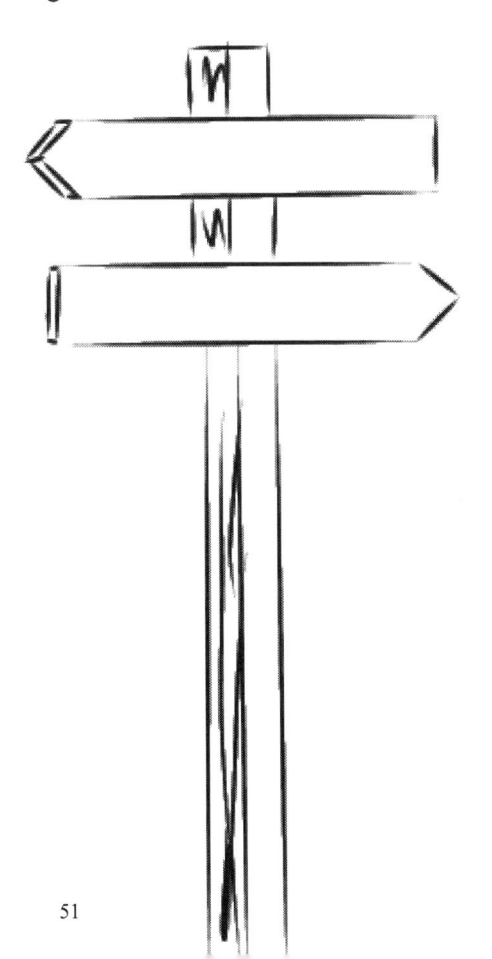

Self Transcending

Every morning, this lady dressed in all black stops the haste of everyday life, and takes a moment to stare at the void.

Sometimes I'm that lady.

Sometimes I'm that void.

I can just detach of any flesh
and embrace the hollowness,
exist like an incomprehensible entity,
desolate in the realms of metaphysics.
On those days, the outside doesn't matter.

But I don't know which is worse and which is better:
own the fact that you have yet to fill the empty,
or ignore it, like others do,
just observe it, like the lady,
but pretend it isn't there.

And then go on with your life like you haven't seen
that it's just a mirror showing what's within.

Somebody told me about tomorrow,
                             and it gets better.

I couldn't tell if he was a fortune-teller,
but I believed
cause nothing can top the sorrow that I feel today.

I hope this pain gets recognized
                        by Guinness World Records
and never gets dethroned
by another episode of mine,
I pray.

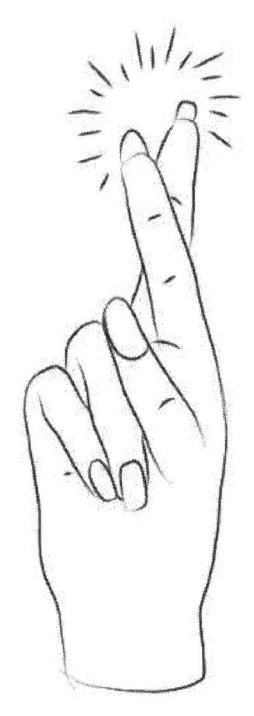

Self Transcending

People don't appreciate my devotion.

My effort is flatlined,
it keeps a high constant rate,
while the only constant in theirs is the decline.

I get less and less till I'm left with crumbs
                              and then goodbyes.

But I got the memo now, it's notable.

It was easy for them to let go
                              of something disposable.

I need a hand.
Someone help me do the right thing cause it feels so wrong.

To be bewildered. To resemble pain with love. To waste your time. To try to restore a feeling that already went down the water pipe. To hang onto something that became moldy. To keep stabbing yourself over and over again trying to save someone else. To disappoint yourself. To keep drinking the poison even after discovering the side effects.

To not wanna lose him.

To not wanna suffocate either.

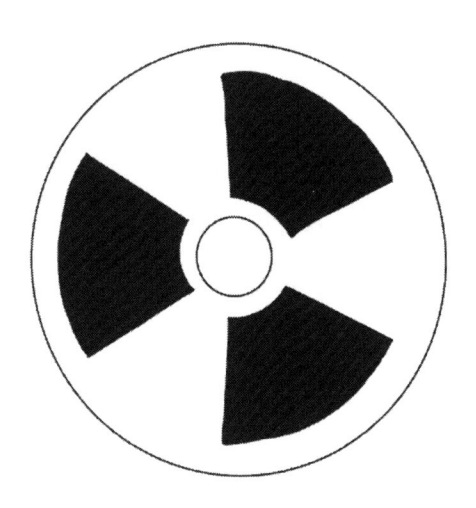

I was forced to face something I never wanted to face,
but you had already found a substitute to play with.

I must learn to embrace this kind of solitude
cause it was hard to let you go
when every inch of me screamed, **"stay!"**

- separation -

I no longer want anything of yours.
The deficit you provoked
in my economy is inconceivable,

you withdrew my love with no remorse.

Wish I could've backed down
when I ended up in point zero,
but that wasn't achievable,
I'm not one to master self control.

I kept on betting on a lost cause,
and I let you take it all.

I'm not holding you accountable,
you only did what you were taught,
and I'm now left empty-handed,
but that's not even the worst part...

Once again, I threw my trust up in the air
and left it where it landed -
not a novice, but disappointment is still hard to bear.

I can take so much more than physical pain.

Your words cut me to the flesh,
and you hurt me to the core,
but I still come back for more,

yet you still give me less
                than I deserve.

Perhaps I want to develop immunity
to my only weakness.

I am the advocate of escapism
cause *the raw reality could use some polishing,*
      but I'm not the practical type.

I find solace in the realm of avoiding,
hiding behind ideas that could bring life
to a soulless body,

but I'm unable to connect them to the physical world.

Self Transcending

I see their eyes flashing in the darkness,
but I pretend they don't exist.

I pretend that these monsters don't cohabitate this vessel,
that these demons don't feel at home in this body of mine.

But the lie doesn't last long
cause I know, I'm not in control yet.

I wish I was.
I wish I could tame them.
I wish I could moderate my emotions.
I wish I could make peace with my shadow self.
I wish I could heal my inner child.

She got off at the next station - <u>Purgatory</u>.
After time of contemplation in solitary,
a rebirth spurred by revelations awaited her.

Cause in this interim place to live
that provides service for a pay,
she'll heal completely
                but leave the past on the counter.

Instead, peace of mind will find her after the passing
cause there is nothing to remind her of what she had
endured anymore.

- Safe Passage on your journey,
Your sins are washed away -

Healing takes forever.

The person I was
and the person I am now
represent two different lifetimes.

I have already died
and have already been reborn.

I've managed to survive,

and now

I am so ready to live.

My life is full of unfulfilled promises.

I remember every,
"we will be together forever, I'll never leave you,"
never hurts any less,

but one thing will always be truthful,
one promise will never get old.
I know and knew it
from the moment it was told,

me and *I* will be together forever,
I knew it from the start,
I will never leave *me*,
not till death do us part.

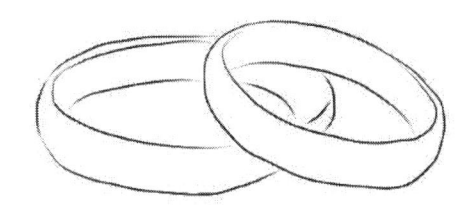

Life takes an interesting turn
when all your convictions are shaken to the ground...

You wouldn't have ever guessed it will come to this.
The recent events were once improbable,
that's why predictions are now doomed,
cause nothing works as it did before,
everything is possible.

Universal laws are now renewed,
'normal' has lost its initial significance,
but change can also be good.

-a revelation at the end of times-

You can learn what your values are,
focus on what matters,
although nothing does that much anymore
      when your world is in tatters.

- living through a global pandemic -

My desire to bounce back - *incontestable.*

I've been in low spirits long enough,
if I stay a minute more, I could develop a habit,
a guilty pleasure
for the sorrow I have to carry with me always,
like an inmate obeying the law and order
of the self-made miserable prose...

I could use a dose of happiness in my unfortunate existence...

The thing is,

    no one knows how to recover,

but, I guess, I have no choice.
I could never abdicate from my position,
and surprisingly, I'm filled with hope.
I am certain I have a mission,
I just have to heal before.

- quarantine revelations -

I'm letting go of contemplation.
Although it once helped me redefine my borders,
lately,
it only brought me isolation from myself and others...

In this silent process,
of continuous fabrication of the self,
I've actually forgot about the beauty of being raw,
of living in the now,

of being...

                    without overthinking...

We're not universal pieces of puzzles,
we are not supposed to fit wherever.

Don't stay where you don't belong,
where there's no need for endeavors,
just because you grew up there,
because there is more convenient.

You should know
        you will not flourish,
where there's no place for your opinion,
where people see right through you,
and your worth is not remarked,

but know that you'll find your home,
if you have the courage to depart.

- about transcending -

Learn to overcome your limiting beliefs.

I know it's hard to grasp that you're spectacular,
> but it's the truth.

I know you're taught to blend in with others,
that being lucky is improbable,
or reaching a prodigy's level of success is implausible,
> but you can blow their minds too.

Walk past the borders society conceived for you,
and you will see much more beyond the horizon.

Join my cult
of insincere friendships
and pretended love,
we strive
to lose our time carelessly.

Throughout my life,
this was an invitation I've been offered repeatedly
from people that I mistook as friends,
loved ones or more.

Because of the play that never ends,
their masks glued onto their core.

I've never shaken their hands,
never mumbled "yes,"
but rather cut the ties.

We split,
and I tried to protest
for a greater cause,
an honest life, and a free spirit.

Hide your face so the world would never find you.

They couldn't possibly comprehend your value,
so stop waiting for someone to understand

> when *you already do*.

I am crawling on my knees,
yet I would never agree to give in,
to stand still.

A source that emanates strength,
I exist.

Therefore, I must fight until
    I no longer have a beating heart,
        or love to give
            to the people that threw mud
            at the one who fought for peace.

- a letter from war -

In between these rows of people,
a few stand out.

But not me
        cause it's hard to distinguish myself -
        I have yet to find my authenticity.

Society already set standards for everyone,
it imprinted values in our brains,
        so it takes a lot to cut off your roots and fly away,
        to estrange yourself from all that you had known,
        to reset your life and rebuild it all alone.

- acknowledgements -

I want to surrender,
to lay down my weapons.

I know nothing but the struggle
cause I was born on the battlefield.

Although I was never a deserter,
this time,
> I'm not sure if these wounds can be healed
> through war...

I have to recall self-love
before I return to the front line.

Self Transcending

I long for the quiet,
>> that soothing silence in my mind
>> that comes by once in a while.

I wish it would stay longer,
so I wouldn't have to ponder every second of the day.
I wish I would find that stillness,
>> but it doesn't come that easily, I guess.

I'd have to silence that explosion of thoughts
made by the loudest parts of my brain
and accept the uncertainty of life...

It's a hard thing to obtain.

- going with the flow seems hard to me -

A never-ending transit,
my life has been.

To belong somewhere is my intention,
so I'm constantly on a journey to another point in space,

pushing forward,
> but never arriving anywhere
> cause I'm stuck in between,
> but at least,
>> I'll leave a trace.

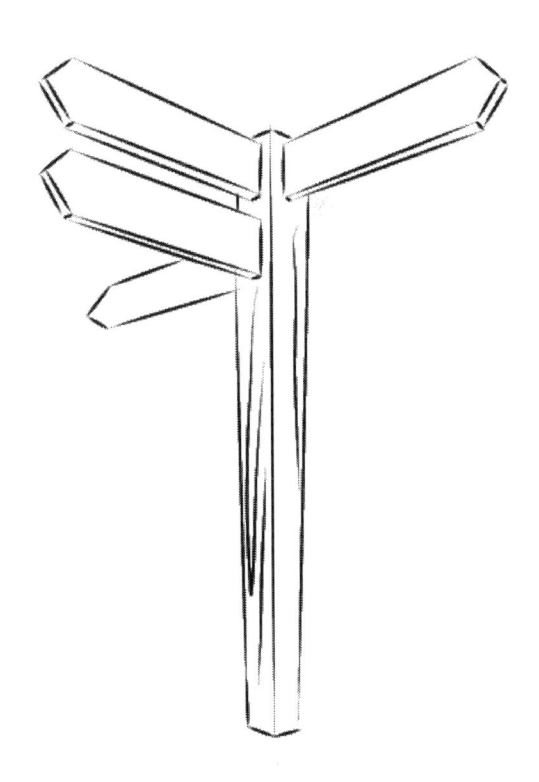

Self Transcending

You have 5 minutes left to live.

Release everything
that has been dragging you down since the beginning.

Take 5
    to let go of generational trauma, a heritage not worth keeping,
    to forget the disgrace you received from peers during your unfortunate high school years,
     to liberate yourself from memories that still sting - you don't have to cling to them.

I actually tried this exercise,
and I realized I found myself
during the 5 minutes break
cause I tried to get out of my head and be awake and present;
        now I'm focusing on pleasant instead.

My childhood was the free trial of my life,
quite appealing, it's good marketing for later.
But, suddenly, a message box pops up:

"Choose your payment method: effort, commitment, or something better."

Now everything comes with a price.

Self Transcending

I'm afraid to fall,
to trip over something,
to ruin what I had.

That's why I stall for time,
I hold on to every second that could be used for leaping,
in the hopes that I'll magically gain some kind of courage,

but in the end, all this sums up to my disadvantage
cause I already know,

if you're waiting all your life,

you won't ever go.

Balance is all I ask for right now.
I'm exhausted from the journey,
always oscillating from one extreme to another,

some days on rock bottom,

                      others on the ladder.

Self Transcending

You are the revolution.
You're shaking the whole world with your power.

And they've been moved by your howl,
your battle cry.
They can resonate with you,
you empower people.

So you have to keep fighting your battle,
                              it's your duty,
no matter how harsh is the struggle,
                              you can do it.

We are waiting for your breakthrough,
it's approaching.

We ventured into something that is passed our level of comprehension -
    we were meant to find each other,
    we tried it since our conception.

But I'm not sure the world is strong enough now
to hold us at the same time.

Both conceived from fire,
we cannot deny the attraction,
but it's *mad:*
Mutually Assured Destruction.

- madly in love -

Self Transcending

I was good on my own,
but you forced your way in –

you took off the door
        and the wall crumbled with it,

yet I couldn't have complained about that,
the mess was worth enduring
cause I never felt that kind of freedom before.

It was more than what I possibly could've wished for.

The scenarios that I play in my head,
like a professional film producer,
damage my clear thinking.

I mistook my feelings for the truth,
and I keep missing
       the remainder that we live in reality.

I hang onto hope,
but here,
       the only thing you feel for me is ruth.

You can't please everyone indeed,
But you were undoubtedly blind then,
you couldn't see me as I am.

Self Transcending

Oh, *little firefly,*
how did you brought back the fire in my soul?

That weak flame is enough for me
cause in the darkest of nights,
       it resembles the sun,

and even though I'm prone to suffering,
       I know there's a flickering out there,
       a gleam that convinced me –
       miracles are happening.

I enjoy being a traveler, but, when I met you, I felt like staying.
It was like the world stopped rotating, and I finally found my stillness,

for a moment, till it ended...

Little did I know you can't play with Universal Laws –

Earth must continue its motion,

so should I.

- you'll find stillness within –

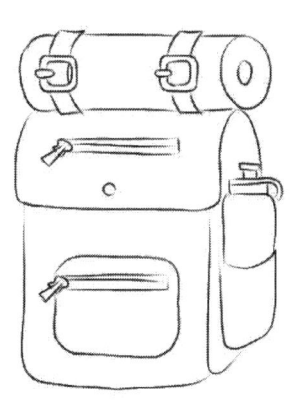

Truth has settled this.
The ultimate arbitrator.

I learned to always embrace it,
        no matter how harsh.

- I won't sweeten my life with a lie ever again -

- wishful thinking -

Could feelings ever be preserved?
It may be an excessive demand,
but I'm not yearning to revive his love,
or relive their friendship,

I'm longing to be awake when I need a hand,
       and the only help I'd seek to be already within.

I want hope to be a practice mastered
through recurrent excitement
and this peace to grow roots inside of me,

       I want to be self-reliant.

Go be an addict.

But choose your addiction wisely.

I'd suggest vitality -
a great daily stimulant for the body and the mind.
Trust me,
> you'll find your new reality irreplaceable.

Oh! to be lively...

To find everything exciting and attainable.
To spill cheerfulness and joy all around.
To feel proud of anything that you achieved or failed.
To not bail on difficult.
To feel hardship worth enduring and life worth living.

I'm surrounded by loss from my past,
but from now on,
       it can only get better.

I saw something shimmering in the distance,
       the only source of light in days.

Got closer so I could identify the matter:
       the reflection of my future is lighting my way.

Self Transcending

Failure isn't for me what it is for someone else,
I am not familiar with its traditional definition.
Every time I fail,
                      I gain.
It's my own form of motivation.

In no time,
                      you'll be giving me ovations.

In the midnight hour, you acquire sensitivity.

You say my gibberish brings you peace of mind,
and the way I stutter helps you recover from your
undeniable dejection.

But when the day breaks,
        you close the blinds,
        push forward retreat,
        and attempt to split us apart,
        saying you don't deserve it,
but you forgot we already pressed start on our connection,

I commit.

Let me assist to your resurrection
cause you're not one of the damned,
and trust me,
        I understand,

so let me help.

Self Transcending

As imperfect beings,
we keep failing to even the scale of affection,
and I'm usually the one
who gets the shorter end of the stick.

I used to believe that you don't value our connection,
but I concluded that

symmetry cannot be man-made,
    so I'm gonna give you my all

        no matter what I get.

The smartest person I know, the one that I loved,
you inspired me to look above and beyond,
to be unconventional.
You showed me how magical everything was,
so I still consider our bond nothing but essential.

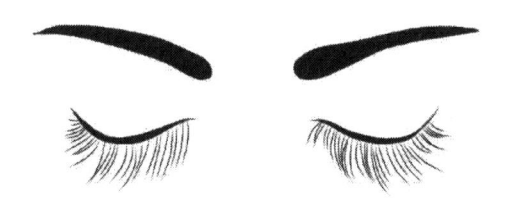

You sparked my revelation.
I'm everything that I am because of you.
I reconsidered my behavior through contemplation,
an experience I'd never undo.

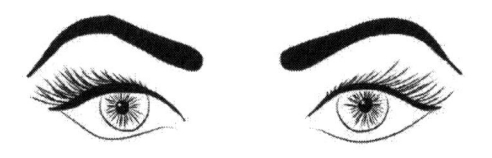

But you didn't follow through on your promise,
you hurt me and disappointed us both.
Still, there won't ever be a time when I'll regret it,
you were a must for my growth.

Self Transcending

Your omnipresence haunts my mortal existence -
you're there,
> yet everywhere I go.

It's like I'm blind
> to anything that isn't you.

If only I could get a sense of how to leave you behind,
> but I can never follow through
> cause you also inhabited my mind.

And, every second, I'm reminded -
> you're in my heart too.

Everything about you has its magic,
and I'm not trying to present to you a fictional prose.

I wish your light could emerge so you'd take a glimpse,
and the monster in your head would decompose.

This is just purely utterly tragic,
that you can't see the most marvelous living thing,
      when it's so close.

If you're gonna waste my time,

                        waste it right.

Fill it with irreplaceable memories
that will sting when you leave.

Make me feel alright,
        even for a little while.
Make me believe in the bright parts of living
        before you lead me in the dark.

But even if our expectations for the future will be deceiving,
for the first time,
 I wanna feel it,
                      not only imagine,
I wanna see it all, take a glance,

I wanna love and be loved once.

Emotionally bruised
and mentally scarred,
barely above the water.

To all this, I was used,
        but you'd be my favorite part
        cause we'll have had
        telepathic understanding
        and meaningful chatter.

        Our connection would be outstanding.

So, this is worth it all,
for the one single encounter.

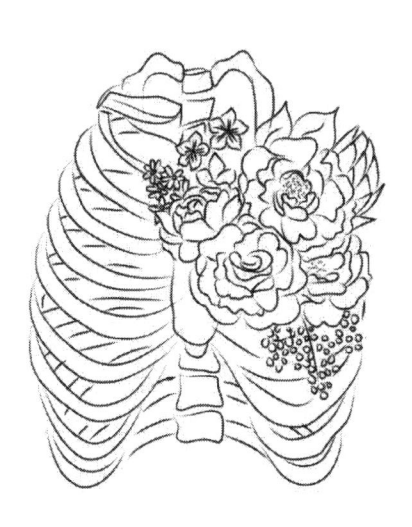

Self Transcending

The mistakes that I made,
the trail of blood spilled by my past self,
and the stains imprinted on my hands
scare me to this day.

I completely deserved your hate
for all the pain that I caused you in my unconscious state.

Numbness took hold of my body,
so leaving your heart shattered felt like a hobby,
but now I'm awake.

Dear self,
    I will never treat you that way ever again.

- alter ego -

Child, don't you be frightened.

Strength resides in you.
There is proof in what you went through
cause you've withstood it all back then
and you've been doing it over since.

You overcame all those tornados,
this mere breeze won't make you flinch.

Self Transcending

I was here.
I can see my memories in this place
like they're holograms.

But have I left a mark behind? A trace?
Cause that's the most important part:
to last,
        even if you're no longer there physically,

to have parts of you spread around
in people's souls,

to abound them.

You are a distant memory.

When I leave this town, you won't be my keepsake
cause I don't want to keep anything
that kept depreciating me on any occasion.

I only remember about you,
how you used to undervalue what I am,
        and that's not worth recalling.

How it took me a long duration
to have a revelation about this,
I still wonder...

But I don't have to ponder anymore,
I have my resolution:

        you're no longer welcomed here.

Self Transcending

You tried to hold me down,
when I was flourishing.

But I'm not gonna contain myself anymore,
not gonna diminish my personality
to reach your level of tolerance.

Why you seem concerned?
Is it cause I earned so much courage?

Mischievous figures crawling from the underground,
they inhabited a world I don't recognize.
I can't identify with any of them
cause they deceive the crowd in attempts to win a prize,
and I tried to give them understanding,
but then it all came with a price
        that I can't afford now,
            nor want to pay anymore.

Keep your wicked lies away from my surroundings.
Perhaps you are evil at your core
cause I doubted anyone could ever
exploit my compassion in such a way,
                imagine my reaction.

I just pray for your salvation,
it would be your benefaction.

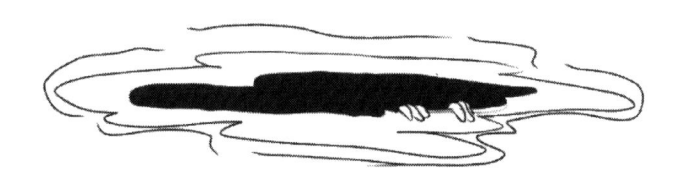

Self Transcending

This has happened all before.
deja vu.

It all seems reoccurring, it's a pattern,

and I'm honestly looking forward to something new,
but repeated cycles will keep appearing till I learn.

I really wish I could discern bad habits from the actual wants.

- why I shouldn't come back to you -

If you're that interested in what I do for a living...
Well...I'm a breather.
And I'm pretty good at it, to be honest.
inhale.
exhale.
inhale.
exhale.
and then repeat.

Hard work for developing skill.

But how could I focus on my job,
       when disappointing people kills?

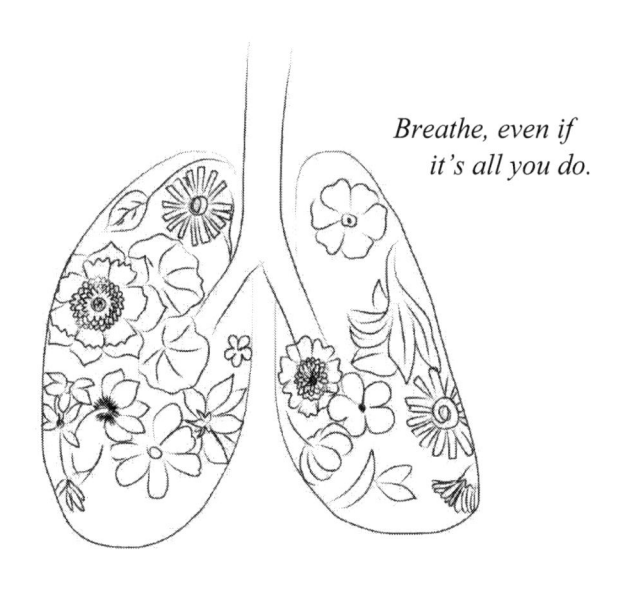

*Breathe, even if
it's all you do.*

There is no right or wrong on their own,
there are only combinations of them.

- mutually inclusive -

Welcome to my madness.
Take a seat near my obsessions.
Have dinner with my neurosis,
and then go to bed with my psychosis.

Love me not,
cause I'm not deserving of your time.

You cannot save me,
only I can.

Self Transcending

I've become a messenger for the greater good.
They whisper in my ear,
and I put it all on paper.

In a hurry to spread the New World Order,
sometimes I save it for later,
often I just repeat it over
in my head.

Do you feel what I'm feeling?
Do you hear them screaming too?

This is chaos,
        but I carry it so you don't have to.

The curtains are now drawn,
so I have to accustom to the blinding lights.

I aspire to clearly see the fabrications,
cause I have no temptation on getting anywhere near them.

I managed to find my authenticity,
so I cannot pretend anymore:
I'll never have an affinity for shallowness,

I wanna pry my heart open for those that are real,
but for the fake ones,

my chest is sealed.

I crave a moment, no matter how short,
when loneliness won't be part of my constitution.

I admit:
        I feel it everyday.

Started to think my condition has no solution,
that I would never feel at peace.

Misfit,
but it costs nothing to hope,
so I'm still waiting for it.

Who pulled the plug on my light?

But a better question is,
why is there still darkness?

Why did I decide I'm not worth the exposure
and kept hiding in the night?

I think I might have become comfortable in the shadows
after you took off,

but I don't need closure to shine.

They told me, *"you have to fit a mold,"*
but I could not find a match,
so I created my own:
>   volatile,
>   as the weather.

Some days I don't like me,
sometimes it's better.

Still finding who I am,
searching, trying on traits
that I could portray,
I keep what I like,
and throw what I hate.

I had so many delays and detours on this journey of mine,
but the final destination is set in stone,
and I'll arrive there on my own,
> no matter the struggles,
>> no matter how many battles I have to win.

Cause I'm not a quitter,
in fact, my goals are getting bigger and bigger each day
since I departed,

and I can die when I'm done,

> but I'm just getting started.

- the nowhere boy -

You could see me spending time with hundreds,
only some
        had ever wondered where I live.
Less burdens for me to handle
cause they'd have probably just end up lost in the woods.
Yet none
        has ever stepped near my empire,

but the gates are higher than the sky,
and the guards have no desire to bring travelers in:

'This is no temporary territory,
you're not welcomed to pass by.
I don't need to check the inventory,
there's no free chair for you to occupy.
You could meet on other journey,
but till then, you shall walk on.'

Been sowing the seeds without any objections
or even interventions
cause I got a worker's life:

I got no time for distractions,
my main intention is to find directions
to a clear ascension,
> perhaps in a superior dimension,
> where there is a possibility for perfection
> cause, until now,

> living in my body felt like detention -
> not being able to experience a thing.

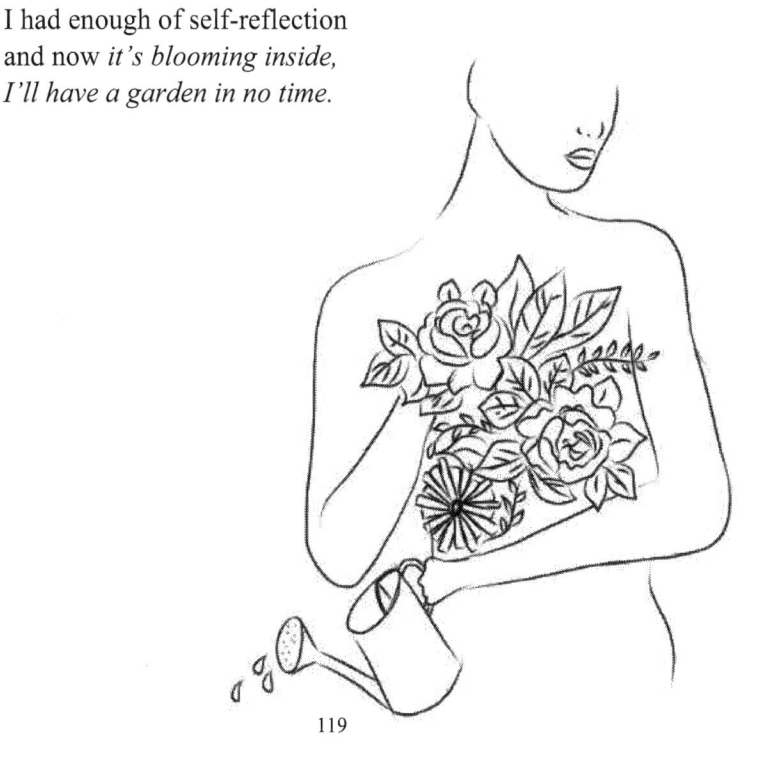

I had enough of self-reflection
and now *it's blooming inside,*
I'll have a garden in no time.

Self Transcending

Life is a blessing, yet a disaster
                in the hands of beginners,
the ones who haven't managed to master
                its subtleties yet.
But, I bet,
                you'll learn to live it properly.

Not by choice.

But by need.

To feed the burning desire that lies within,

to firmly say,
                "I lived."

Every morning I wake up with this longing in my chest,
struggling to remember something that I simply cannot
grasp.

I keep on forgetting.

A thing,
or a name,
or a meeting in the astral plane

that bears so much importance,
       of this, I am sure.

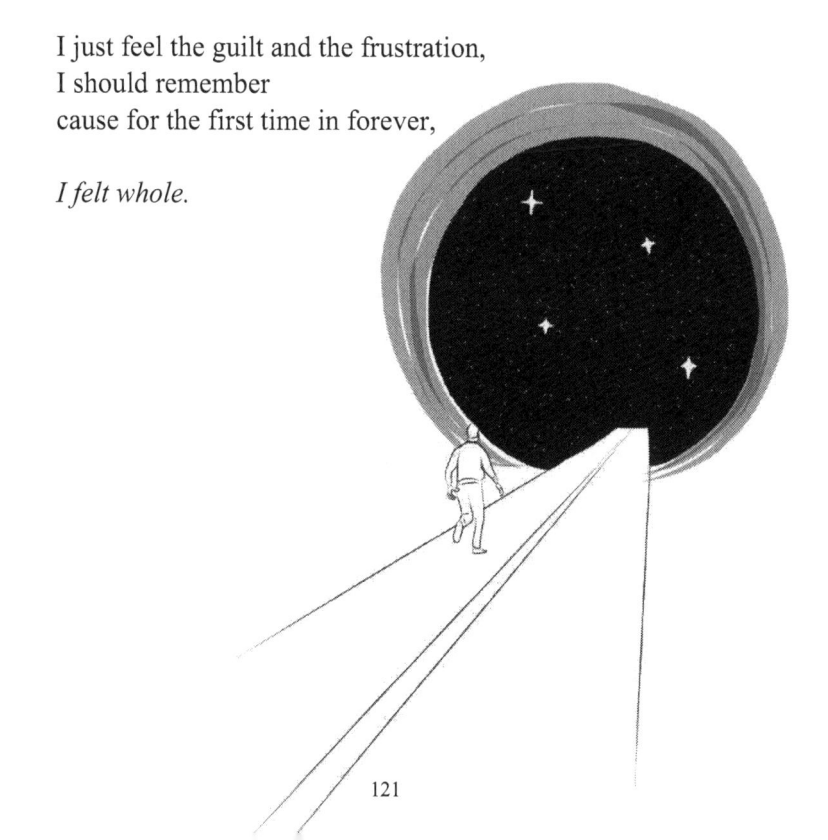

I just feel the guilt and the frustration,
I should remember
cause for the first time in forever,

I felt whole.

Stop blindly maintaining the status quo,
be intentional.

Do what you love,
and live an unconventional life, if you want to.

Take space in this world,
be dimensional and unapologetic about it.

You had your hardships but pulled through like a professional,
and you became unbelievably exceptional;
I really wish you could see all of it.

I've been fighting my insignificance since the beginning of times. I struggled to be heard in all that noise. I suffered from being see-through in a world belonging to elites.
I was never one of them. *I've been incognito my whole life.* I hung out with the so-called "dregs of society". I didn't belong to them either. An outsider, that's what I was.

But the solitude brought me inner peace. And I rose from the bottom. Now everybody is watching.

Paradise

It all makes sense for her now.

Cause, as Dante knew,
to reach Paradise you have to go through Hell first,
otherwise, you couldn't possibly tell what happiness
really feels like.

For life is composed of antitheses:
you had to tame the chaos to find peace,
you needed to feel the pain to feel love in its enormity,
you had to accept your shadow self in order to stand in
the light,
you had to experience in order to understand in depth.

But the painful journey has come to an end
cause you're on a high vibration now.

Dear child, meet your true, *higher self.*

Self Transcending

Always on the lookout for the unknown,
I don't have an idea of what I'm searching for.

But every new piece discovered,
        helps me see it, it's fascinating,

a life continuously enriched
        till all the secrets become uncovered,
        infinite knowledge, it's breathtaking.

*Forgive me, spirit,
for forgetting about you.*

I was indulging my body in luxury
and neglected to care for you too.
A loyal follower of materialism, I was,
because of the blind adaptation to the mass,

> but I managed to pass
> in a higher state of mind.

> I'm kind, not to my body,

>> but to my essence.

I am surrounded with the consequences
of my own mistakes.
The world is in a hurry to put a tag on me
and all I could say is,

*"Excuse me for the inconvenience,
it's my first time living."*

My truth is my own,
but I'll respect yours
as long as you don't try to shove it down my throat.

You cannot brainwash me,
your efforts are in vain.

What are you attempting to sell?
Are you trying to convince me
                              or yourself?

What you want is yours already,
$\qquad\qquad\qquad$ you attract it.

The pieces fit perfectly till your wish is granted
cause the odds are in your favor,
but you have to believe.

- law of attraction -

I want to know you.
I want to sail in your mind,
through undiscovered parts.

I want to land then in your permanent memories,
like your consciousness has become my home,
like I'm one of your automatisms too,

and you don't have to remember me any longer
cause, now, I'm part of you.

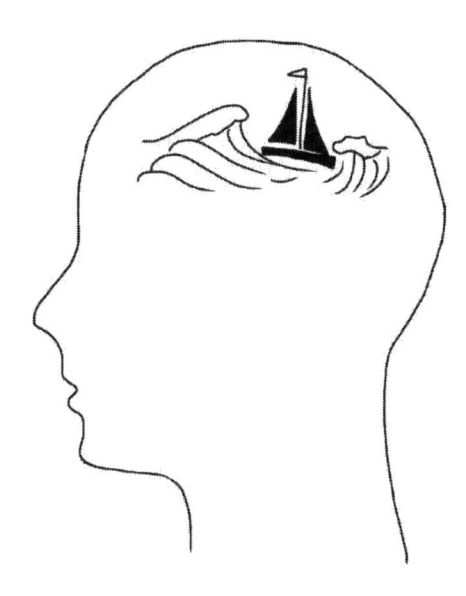

The vibrations of your voice got imprinted in my brain
after you shared with me your truth.

At night, my mind repeats them like a lullaby,
and this sound makes me die and come to life
at the same time.

But in the midst of chaos, you are my safe haven.
I don't even have to call you mine.
I'm blessed to even breathe the same air
or see the view of something so divine.

You are purely ethereal.

Then, there was you.
I found love in the most unexpected of places,
in a time of surrendering all hopes.

You picked them up and pushed them higher,
convinced me that I can acquire everything.

"You're in the wrong, my love; you're born to be extraordinary,
don't settle for the ordinary.

When lost, I'll be your guidance,
push you through till your strength heightens.

I'll stand beside you on your worst
and be the one to cheer you on
until the moment that we're gone."

Self Transcending

I saw a unique shade in you,
like all the colors had already been used
on others,
       so you had to improvise.

I realized you had a distinct voice,
like your initial frequencies
had been altered,
       so you became this specific sound
       anyone could recognize,
       no one could mistake.

You felt different,
like an electric current
with a tint of love.

Honestly, nobody could dethrone you from above.

Attachment is said to come gradually,
but we redesigned the facet of love,
although we sculpted without pottery lessons.

We were guided from the start.
Our connection - work of art.

This is my confession:
I felt nothing and then felt it all at once
cause I recognized you at first glance.

We've met at the beginning of times,
but got separated by the cycle of life,
so we had been trying to reach each other for a while.

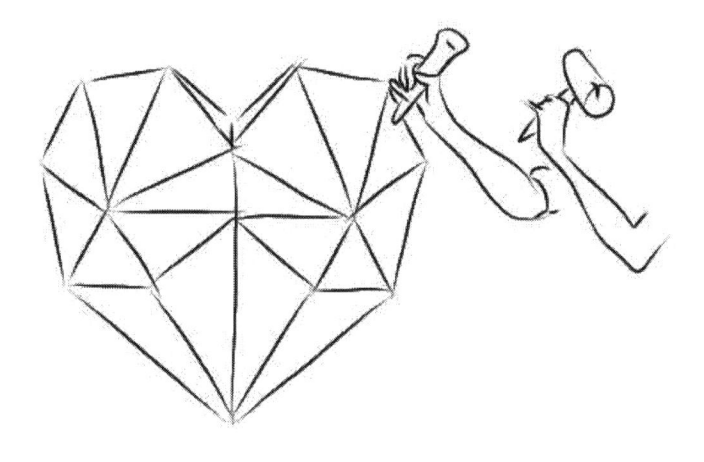

You are always filled with kindness.
Sometimes it overflows
and you spread it like rays, all around.

How can someone take the place of the sun?

Never met an angel on the ground
until now.

There are people in this world
who have incorporated in my soul.

The marks on my body hold
the spot of their fingerprints.

They're part of me
and forever will be,
I cannot erase them
and I'll never try to.

I stood behind the curtains way too long,
waiting for my debut show,
overanalyzing,
overthinking,

but it was only when I decided to deliver impromptu
that the world became my stage

cause it only takes a few seconds of courage,
a little resilience,
and a definite risk
for a rewarding life experience.

You said you wanna keep me close
cause I brighten your darkest days,
but you forgot
that I'm just a reflection of your light,

you're the one bringing to life

pure radiance.

Self Transcending

Lonesome but crowded,
boring and complex,
take it as it is, but change it,
model your life as you please.

Cease
        to see yourself as a victim.

You have within a latent fire
and near you
is everything you desire,

    so live!

I want to know everything,
a genius of it all I want to be.

It's not a matter of pride or fame,
it's a calling that I can't forsake.

Venture into the unknown,
just for the sake of it.

Self Transcending

I was born to succeed,
to exceed expectations about me.

I've already proven my worth,
but you still don't get it.

Can't you see?

I'm not just ambitious, daring,
        although it's true,

                I am limitless,

no words can define what I can do.

My dear lost friend,
I need to show gratitude more often.

We parted ways long ago,
but you built me whole with your compassion,
and your weird jokes that made me laugh
gave me long-lasting satisfaction.

Our memories can't be erased,
and, be sure, you're not replaced,

you're in my heart, and I'll be there,
when you need a word of kindness,
when they just keep throwing dirt,
if you have no one to go to,

I'll care,

        I'll always do.

My hopes are as high as the distance between Land and sky.

"Don't risk it, you won't be able to do it," they say.
 But I can try.

Either way,
    the decision is all mine,
so stop throwing with opinions everywhere.

I won't let anyone but the Universe itself
change the grande finale of my life.

So you won't influence the outcome,
    you are only wasting time
cause I don't listen to voices intended to scare me away,
they come from a place of envy and settling for less,
    and I already know what's best for me:
I cannot stay in the comfort zones,
    I have already outgrown them.

Ordinary people with ordinary ideas
and a society
that expects you to fall in line.

Don't conform to the norm, be the outlier
cause you were born for so much more
than what you see within this barrier.

If people call you insane, just say you agree
cause it's this madness that you possess
that's really setting you free.

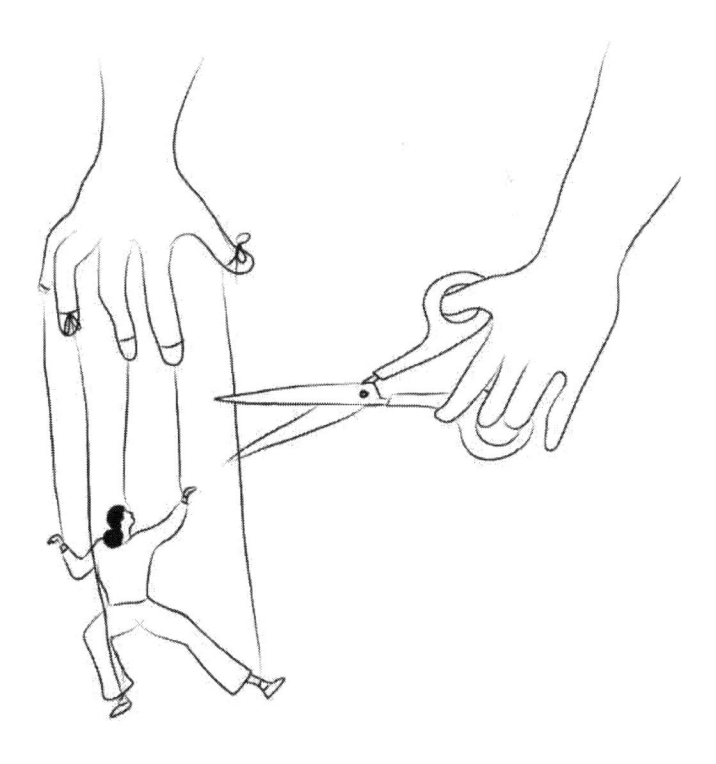

Self Transcending

Casually sitting in your bad pile
cause I'm not one to obey.

I'm the one who steps on the wrong tile,
I won't get out of the way,
        so they get irritated.

But I've got things to say,
        and not many have the guts to,
so I'm gonna make myself heard.
One way or another,
you're gonna listen to every word…

They say I'm a bother,
so, occasionally, the burden weighs a lot,

but I rather not stay quiet,
        and I will never be compliant
              with something morally unjust.

I got over your betrayal.

So now it's *payback time:*

> I'll show you kindness and let you be,
> I won't avenge my broken heart.

Cause I don't do "revenge," it's beneath me.

I wish you farewell,
although you never justified your actions,
and I never knew about *'why'* or *'how',*

but tit for tat is a child's game,
and we're all grown up now.

- completely healed -

Self Transcending

If you ever crossed my path,
you're never leaving
without a trace on my soul.

A life-long pact,
        that's what friendship is for me.

We're more than acquaintances,
we're souls bond by connections, you see,
you will be remembered forever,
as a part of me.

This bond that we created through hardships of our own,
priceless.
Every sorrow shared with one another,
every heartbreak that made us closer to each other
convinced me I'll never feel alone ever again,

this friendship is timeless.

And the silly things, the inside jokes,
the awkward moments, the joyful ones,
they made me feel at home.

Little did I know,
we built a family of our own.

- *soul tribe* -

Your efforts don't go unnoticed, mom.
You sacrificed your well-being since the moment
I was born,

and I have seen
how you kept me warm when you were freezing,
how you fed me while you were starving,
how you showed me love when you felt like dying.

But that's only the bare minimum,

you did so much more.

You spoiled me when I was greedy,
and I demanded the world,
yet you never failed to deliver,
even when you struggled to make ends meet.

I could never fully compensate you for what you did
cause you're a miracle worker,
and I am just *a kid*.

But God should save you a front seat in Heaven.

- blessed -

Let's touch each other's hearts while life lasts,
and let us watch the power gained
through our vulnerable discussions
cause you don't have to take precautions anymore,
but I understand your hesitation.

Let me intertwine my fingers in yours.

Love waits.
Love endures.

So, I'll be patient for you while you're cautious.

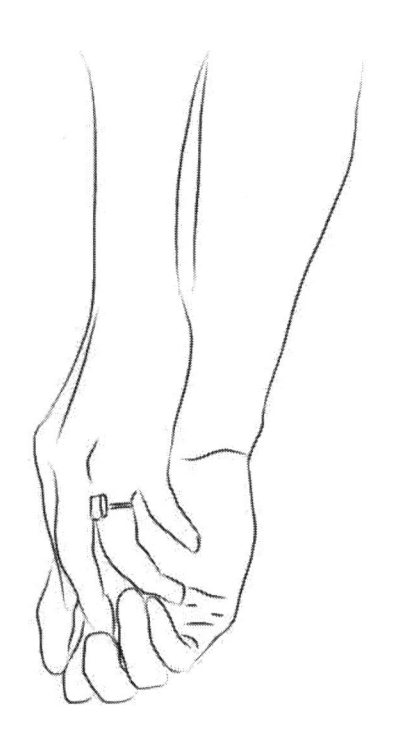

We inherited the conception
that showing our love makes us weak.

I'm gonna be honest,

        today I want to feel *the weakest.*

I want to shout it from the highest building,
let everyone know it's true;
do not think for a second that I'm kidding
when I say that *I love you.*

On the day I met you: serendipity.
A blessing from above, you were,
cause we cured our wounds with love,
and this was never a simplicity for me.

Easiness never felt like home before,
but you invaded my heart,
comprehended every part,
and I finally found someone that *I adore*.

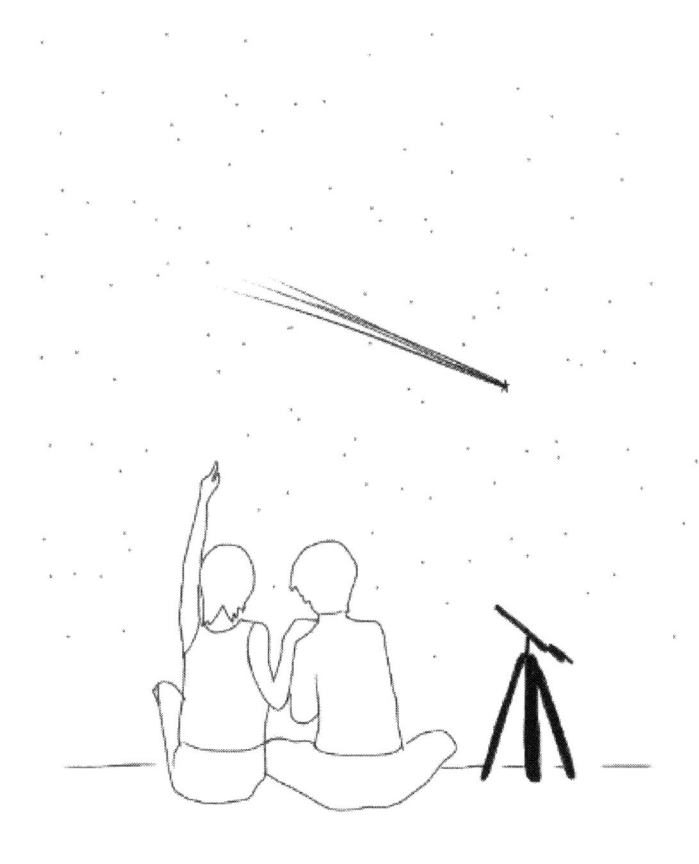

Self Transcending

They wouldn't get our connection, *love*.

They don't have linked wires,
       so they aren't wired to understand us.

It's impossible to perceive
cause, most times,
the only way to see
is through closing your eyes
and letting yourself feel,
and you and I are the only ones blessed
with this capacity.

So, let's forget the rest
cause, in reality,

        we're all we need.

You and I have nothing to lose except each other,
but that's a lot.

I cannot make such a compromise:
        to bargain with everything I got.

You're everything I fought for;
we're one and the same,
I cannot be parted with my twin flame.

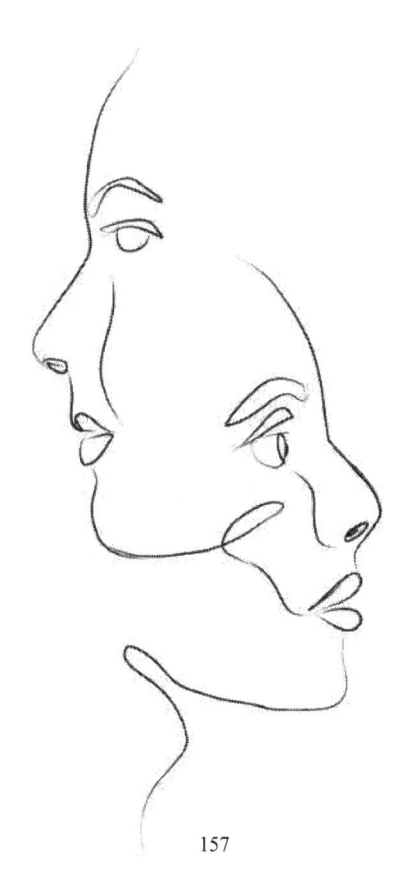

Self Transcending

I became a passenger on this journey involuntarily,
but I'm a wanderer by choice.
I can hear the voice that I carry within
                    begging for new scenery,
so I'm keen to walk away,
but all the emotions that I felt stayed with me.

I can't help but stray away from my surroundings,
but I'm not looking for *'belonging to a place,'*

my place is on the move.

So I can't wait to be astonished once again by this world
that I live in,
by the marvels that I see,
cause there's nomad blood flowing through my veins.

In this lifestyle, all things change,
but *I feel f r e e,*
and that's the one thing that remains.

Been sailing for some time,
lost in the swamp that is my mind, leaving no trace.

But like a lighthouse,
you guided me home into your embrace,
and that's just one of the perks
of being madly in love.

Yet, some say that's how infatuation works:
                it burns but dies out quickly,
                    and you're left with the remains...

That's not the case with our connection,
and they're not to blame
cause they don't see the clear waters you brought in,

only we can recognize this everlasting flame.

I do not care what my social status is
I search through the room
for my soul,
> not for attention.

You can hate me as long as you want,

> I'll survive.

It's just natural selection.

I really felt seen this time.
How was it possible to touch my spirit blindly,
to connect with me through waves of energy?

Well, I found my answer down the line:
we're meant to be.

The whole planetary system supports our synapsis,

who am I to oppose a law of the universe?
I could never sabotage this.

Self Transcending

I'm not confident, I am above confidence.

I wear my colors on display
for people to observe and pray
that someday they'll have the courage to do the same.

I collected every fragment of my broken self
and then I put it back in place,
in a time when my nickname was *'disgrace'*.

Only later had I realized,
I haven't stumbled upon something that I could not face,
and I'm starting to believe there is no such thing,

    I am the embodiment of strength.

Beautiful comes in a million ways.
The way your hair lays down on your shoulders,
the ideal ratio of melanin in your skin,
the impeccable proportions of your body-

All perfectly conceived.

You have nothing to cover,
 it's only beauty I see.

But your inner nature, the way you behave, your
personality blew me away.

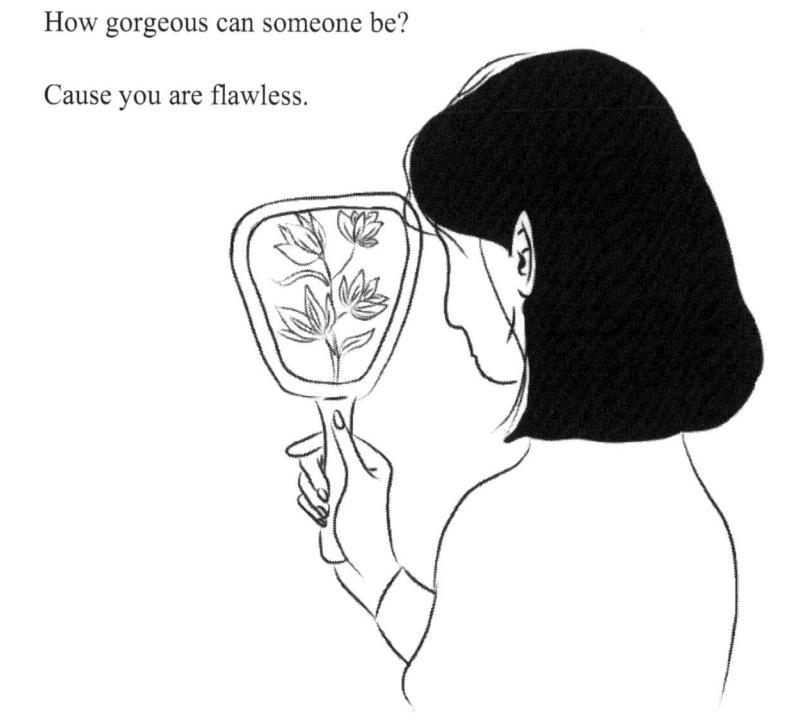

How gorgeous can someone be?

Cause you are flawless.

I let it in,
the knowledge of the wisest
sent to me through divination.

I'm not afraid of the unknown,
I know the direction I have to take,
and I have faith,

my intuition is resounding.

They said even unrequited love has its worth.
I won't pretend, I couldn't quite grasp the idea,

but now I understand.

Love is preserved.

It never gets wasted.
It may be around the curve,
but will eventually come back to where it was created.

Maybe in a different manner,
perhaps after a while,
love will strike and build your world,
but will remind you how to smile.

Self Transcending

I have a dream in me
that seems unreachable to the faint-hearted.

But since it started,
this yearning,
       invisible to the naked eye,
       cannot be tamed
       or contained.

I have to let it out,
to let it be on its own,
and, once that's done,
let us see where it takes me.

I have never known completeness until I met you.

Living my daily routine,
unaware of the magnitude my spirit could achieve,
blindly convinced that I wouldn't want anything but myself.

Don't get me wrong,
I am undoubtedly whole on my own,

but with you,
                I am infinite.

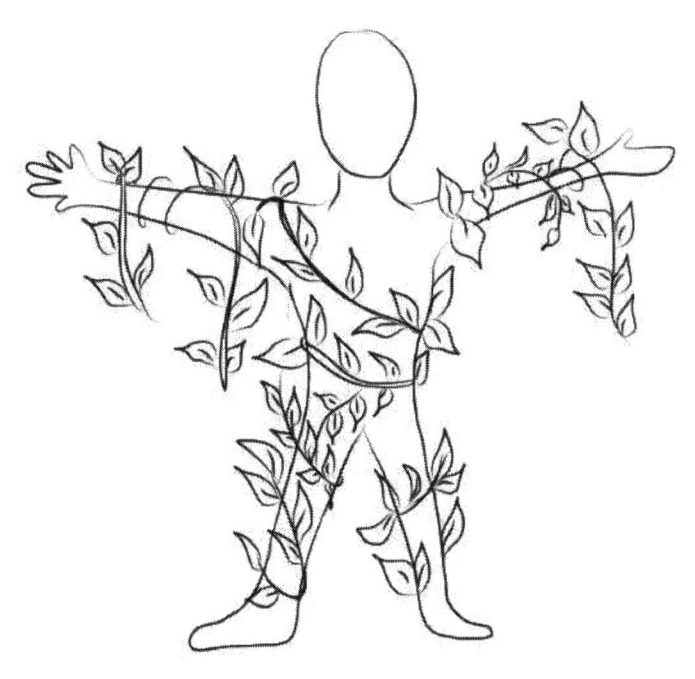

I can't promise you tomorrow,
but today is in our hands.

- I'm not into forecasting; I live in the now -

I've seen Hell,
but some cannot tell that
cause I learned how to carry on and heal the ache
after I went through Purgatory.

But you understand it now,
I told you my story,
and I'm sure you have your own.

A tale, unknown to me, and, perhaps, to others,
but I'm sure your mind wanders at times-
'Why were you born? What is the purpose, if there is one?'
Sure, there are plenty of kinds.
I couldn't possibly particularize and answer for everyone;
you have to discover your very own,
but I can uncover something for you...
We share a goal.
We're not only meant to find Paradise on Earth,
we have to feel it all.

So go on now, be brave, and learn from pain;
it's your turn to gain experience
cause you have crowds to blow away with your resilience.

Made in the USA
Columbia, SC
19 December 2020